# A MONTH OF SOMEDAY

INDOLENT BOOKS

# A Month of Someday

## POEMS

GERALD WAGONER

INDOLENT BOOKS

www.indolentbooks.com
Indolent Books
209 Madison Street
Brooklyn, NY 11216

ISBN: 978-1-945023-30-9

Special thanks to Epic Sponsor Megan Chinburg
for helping to fund the production of this book.

# CONTENTS

# A MONTH OF SOMEDAY

I walk on the shady side.
Fewer people to sidestep.
Spring is the season some
stoops display outgrown
children's books, boxes of
puzzles, games, and dozens
of multi-colored cloth critters
arrayed for passersby to
pick through. Open, empty,
a solitary red Poké Ball
on the sidewalk. Maybe
Mary Shelly, anime monster
in her pocket, gathers fresh
flowers to toss down a well.

The lone patrol car rolls.
A commercial trash truck
idles. Empty trains rattle
below. A stranger quick
draws a bird on brick.

Suspended without suspense,
time is elusive in limbo. Unseen
bottles clink, clatter into some
recycle bin. A woman scrapes
her garbage can to the curb.

No thrum from the great city.
I might be lost in the forest,
slogging through an all white
snowfall, or tied in the twisted
sheets of last night's dream.

Tonight I am with clouds
in the night sky. There
is wind. Halyards knock
the mast. Flags fly west.
I cannot stanch the
dimming city light.
This place, if possible,
feels emptier again.

It is ten, after the rain, when
laughter breaks the silence
of my nightly walk, there,
screened under an unlit
theater marquee, a father,
faux monster, incites two
daughters to frolic, to squeal.
Forget fear. No one is here
to bump when you jump.

Rejoice in your bodies.

Throw off the constricting day
that confined you to rooms
too small to work, to parent,
to grow. It's night beneath
the theater's dark marquee.

Rejoice in your bodies.

There is ample room to run.
No one to run into. Shriek delight.
Dance with shadow and with light.

Rejoice in your bodies.

It is late, but no one near
will chide you for your joy,
nor scold you this dank night
your bright squeals of glee
light up our dark marquee.

Sifted compost
into soil until lunch.
Morning melancholy
dissipated like cloud
cover. I'm ready now
to leave the house
incognito; fedora
pulled down, top coat,
collar up, sunglass,
and veil. Clerks will
not recognize me.
The sexually active,
in general, only see
each other. As for the
spatially challenged?
They, like the biblical
poor, will always be
too close for comfort.

Each car is audible.
To youth I am invisible.
Two middle aged
women drink vodka
on their stoop. Their
greeting, in passing,
sounds too much
like farewell. Venus
gleams tonight.
The moon is Islamic.
It is setting.

In dark and solitude I walk
Prospect West to Grand
Army Plaza, then down
Union to Bond. Pink super-
moon obscured behind
overcast sky. Phantoms
of desire whistle airs to
time passed. I entertain erotic
dreams to feed the ghosts.

A grumble of muffled voices
from a second floor room.

Outside the hospital, a row of
ambulances wait, idling.

Shuttered shops
spawn wind strewn trash.

Someone in shadow,
mad in disappointment,

declaims a poem
of non sequiturs.

Across the canal it echoes
through hollow buildings.

The tide comes in heavy
on yesterday's wind.

The pink moon untangles
itself from still black branches.

The flaccid flag's halyard
taps the pole wearily.

It's the same empty
night after night.

A place in Brooklyn to stand
to watch the stark white moon
rise so round two days late,
and ascend through tangled
branches. In a waning wild,
the world's end on pause,
I am a surprise to myself.

Now is the time. The roots are restive, and I have an abrupt itch
to erect small brick walls. I bought one hundred used bricks, and
two eighty pound bags of dry mortar. I squat. Ponder where the
first course will lie. The clay block, mildly abrasive, fits neatly in my
crane claw hand. Mortar and water are mixed. My trowel is at
ready. Solzhenitsyn's account of the prisoner laying bricks to erect
the walls of his own prison, ennobling the task before me now.

Tomorrow He is risen.
Two meters sounds
closer than six feet
here on this long line.
It's seniors-only-time
at the grocery store.
Life's simple isness
makes living
incomprehensible.
We wait long on line
A man with a bullhorn
begs for our patience.
He is young.
I have less time than
he dreams. Each
year, for years
I tremble this week
in rapt anticipation
for the resurrection
of my beloved
Dove's chocolate
covered, coconut
cream eggs.

On Union street I stop to watch
a pumper truck, able to pump a
thousand gallons of water a minute,
be backed into Squad Company 1
Station House, one of New York's
eight Special Operations Commands.
A carved wooden monument, near
the door, is dedicated to the firefighters
killed when burning towers buried
a world view. I've come to suspect,
since humans first flaked flint, all
treasured gifts of blood and smoke
arose as confessions of impotence.
The wind will not be appeased:
no matter whose child is offered.

Across the Gowanus
the murky echoes of a
past fading. On the Union
Street bridge I adjust
my focus to freeze the
mylar shimmer of big
city light on ruffled water.

My wool coat breaks the chilly,
gusting winds that scud clouds
overhead like once-eager
commuter trains. The sun breaks
bright in gaps. Brooklyn's
ornamental fruit trees blossom
yellow, white, pale pink. Tulips
amaze me in red intensity.
Azalea starbursts excite my
iris. Lilacs bloom either lilac or
white, yet this April, even more
than before, they grow on me.

*—4/15   2 pm 47° Sun and Clouds*

A ladder truck flipping
red and white strobe,

glare, claxons, sirens,
charges full flat out

down empty Smith Street,
up toward Atlantic Avenue.

The uniformed responder's
white, red, or blue lights

fracture our silent nights
into shards of alarm.

Someone, somewhere
is burning, is gasping.

Queued up Trader Joe's.
Funk organ sound track.
A woman wearing black
velour hoodie, legs criss-
crossed, hair drawn back,
a round knot tight on top.
Cubist: all arcs & vectors.

I chatted briefly while
waiting on line outside
the hardware store
with a younger man who
years ago left Iowa
the same way I left
Montana. Both of us
willing to trade more
traffic for a mutable future.

*—4/18    11:00 pm 49° Low Cloud Cover*

When out this late,
cars are rare.
Opposite our local
Nursing Home,
today's town criers
of nightly death sit
in their black news
van sipping cold
coffee from paper
cups. It's the same
night, every night.

The subway rumbles
through down there.
I want to go somewhere,
but sadly, now I'm too
aware, so do not dare.

The Greeks say Agamemnon
so loved his glory he was willing
to sacrifice his virgin daughter.
Though some say Artemis took
Iphigenia, and provided a deer.

The Hebrews say, years later, in
another story, an angel, on the gory
point of filicide, stayed Abraham's
willing hand. Said: it's the thought
that counts. You can use a lamb.

More recently, say the Christians,
a god transcendent entered human
form to weep in frequent anguish,
to dance our fleeting joy, to bleat
against the blade and the void.

—*4/21    9 pm 55° Wind and Rain*

My teacher friend tells
me her team is planning
a marvelous poetry unit.
They will require students
to answer, in poetic form,
all the major questions
of life and living in a
pandemic. I say, go for it,
but personally prefer the
seemingly insignificant.

Early morning I walked
to the hardware store,
then did concrete work.
Filled erosion gaps around
the stoop, patched shift
cracks in the back wall.
Messed with words this
afternoon. Hoped a few
shy figments from sleep
would drift close enough
to the light I might pluck
them from their matte
black fog. They hide like
the trout you know are
there: tight to a big rock,
shielded under reflected
sky. I cast, expectantly,
repeatedly, all my best
lures until it felt more
like a job, than a creek to
be worked again, maybe,
someday in this perpetual
month of somedays.

—*4/23   9:15 pm 52° Scudding Clouds*

Today I vacuumed, scrubbed, mopped
the house. Early in my journey to become
a sculptor I chose to do minimum wage
janitorial work. Daylight was for carving stone,
fluorescent for waltzing gestural expressions
of infinity symbols with an industrial scale mop.

Night is personal. I walk alone. Slink into
shadows. Hear the wind in my head, and
once, the faint tinkle of young revelers drifting
toward the harbor. I remap my route often
to avoid human contact. I'm here to recall the
expressway's raspy hum. Listen to Doppler
effect sirens. Consider breaks and endings.

Night: misty, drizzle.
It's always sunset
on the River Styx.
No cars. WALK WAIT
spills a block's worth
of orange then white
over oil-black bluestone.
I fear this is not yet
as empty as it gets.

I'm one of those who loves
a wall; one of those who
loves a stone's silence; loves
the idea of stone sentences;
each word a unit of exclusion;
this one has been scheming
to pinch a couple of grey
granite cobble stones
found next to the curb
alongside the grade school.
City property. Not in front
of someone's building.
Detached from any retaining
or decorative purpose,
makes it fair game to justify
removing something
not my own, even if it is
a perfect fit to finish a thing
that will outlast me. Time is
getting away. It is raining.
I miss the flesh of friends.

I meet my doctor
on the street. On
The Island some
must hose off cold
naked outside:
deaths, staff sick.

Everyone making
nothing the same
like when you snap
a carpet, disturb
particulate tension.

In the river a wave
through water,
being matter,
is still a wave to
a rug, but not
to the same rug.

Recently, though
some have begun

to spread rumors
of chimerical
plateau indicators.

Grey, rain periodic. Near
the 9th street bridge people
with no firm outlines; their
details sketchy. An athletic
couple jogs past. A flash
of white band underwing.
Many-songed mockingbirds
fill tulip trees. Monet's I think.

There are three
adolescent boys

on a park bench
evenly spaced.

A twinge in my
gut triggers me

to phone an old
traveler, confess

I live too distant,
wait too long.

Too often lately,
on my nightly
walk I make out
a form half in
shadow down
the block.
I'm sure that
she or he waits
on their dog,
but closer it's
the work of
dark and fog.
More clearly
now it appears
to me, certainty
is most certainly
not nearly as certain
as it used to be.

Tonight I came upon two big rigs
parked head to head on the sidewalk
opposite Con Ed. On each lowboy
trailer tons of copper cable
spooled onto five tall, wide wheels.
Each cab sported gleaming chrome,
an array of custom running lights.
Each was painted lustrous white.
Scripture, lettered in silver script
behind the driver's door on one.
It sounded Calvinist, and once
I would have dismissed the driver
an unthinking drone. An enemy
of complex thought. A stranger
to the sceptic's requisite doubt.
But, tonight, I imagine how grand
it must be hauling Interstate 80 from
your Indiana to my Brooklyn.
Up high, maybe the window down,
your elbow out, with what you
believe to be truth hand lettered
meticulously beside you
for all the world to see.

We cannot hold our hands
We must hide our mouths
Must abide our times
Maybe we follow our gut
Maybe pass some revelers
Play with empty words
Want to believe
the lost can return
We hear sirens clear
See blue and red and
white speed into black
sounds that carry
The old floats away
A lost balloon
A message in a bottle
to be finished
on sidewalk in chalk
We all dance the wide
berth shuffle now
with grace
with fluid ease
Still I walk at night
to hillside park

to inky harbor
the surface roiled
the skyline steady

# ACKNOWLEDGMENTS

*BigCityLit*

    4/24 10 pm 50° Misty Drizzle

    4/25 9:18 pm 42° Overcast

*Book of Matches*

    4/1 11 am 47° Sunny

*Brownstone Poets Anthology*

    4 /4 10 pm 45° Cloudy, Light Wind

*Helix*

    4/21 9pm 55° Wind and Rain

    4/22 3:50 pm 54 Cloudy

*Maryland Literary Review*

    4/2 9:10 pm 44° Clear

*Misfits*

    4/6 9:15 pm 48° Clear

    4/14 2 pm 47° Sun and Clouds

    4/17 3:28 pm 50° Sunny

    4/27 3:15 pm 55°

*Night Heron Barks*

    4/12 Easter 10:30 pm 47° Clear, Still

*October Hill*

    4/10 2:40 pm 52° Grey, Light Rain

*Right Hand Pointing*

    4/18 11:00 pm 49° Low Cloud Cover

*Shot Glass*

    4/7 10:25 pm 49° Cloud Cover

    4/28 10:30 pm 42° Light Breeze

*What Rough Beast*

    4/8 9:50 pm 48° Clear

    4/19 9:30 pm 54° Clear

    4/30 9:15 pm 48° Still

*Umbrella Factory*

    4/5 2:10 pm 54° Variably Cloudy

    4/9 9:50 pm 50° Clear

    4/23 9:15 pm 52° Scudding Clouds

THERE ARE MANY PEOPLE I NEED TO THANK for their support and assistance in the shaping of this book. First I want to thank my wife Mari Oshima, and my sons Kai Wagoner-Oshima and Yasu Wagoner-Oshima. You keep me grounded. Thank you Michael Broder, my teacher, my friend, and now also my publisher. Thank you Rachel Hadas for being my teacher, my friend and for writing a blurb that still takes my breath away. Thank you Lisa Andrews for your unbridled generosity of spirit. Thanks to Hilary Sideris for your attentive reading and insightful comments. Thank you Amy Holman for being my guide since the beginning. Thank you Lynn McGee for giving me a place to begin. Thank you Susana H. Case for your long faith in me. And finally, thank you David Formanek, for your meticulous proof reading of my final draft. And I thank each of the editors who published my poems in their journals.

# ABOUT THE AUTHOR

Gerald Wagoner is a poet, teacher, and visual artist. His poems have appeared in *Beltway Poetry Quarterly*, *BigCityLit*, *Blue Mountain Review*, *Book of Matches*, *Cathexis Northwest Press*, *Coffin Bell*, *Helix*, *Maryland Literary Review*, *Night Heron Barks*, *October Hill*, *Right Hand Pointing*, *Shot Glass*, *The Lake*, *What Rough Beast*, and *Umbrella Factory*, as well as in the Brownstone Poets 2022 Anthology, edited by Patricia Carragon. Born in Eastern Oregon, Wagoner went to college in Montana, then headed east and earned an MFA in sculpture at SUNY Albany. He settled in New York City where, after teaching K–6 students as a Studio in a School artist in residence, he went to work for the Board of Education teaching art, language arts, and English as a second language. After retiring from the Board of Ed in 2017, Gerald returned to his youthful passion for poetry. As a sculptor, he has had dozens of shows from 1981 to the present throughout the country and around the world. *A Month of Someday* is his debut poetry collection.

## ABOUT INDOLENT BOOKS

Indolent Books is a poetry press based in Brooklyn. When I started the press in 2015, I did so with the express mission of publishing work by poets over 50 without a first book. I soon expanded the mission to include other kinds of outsiders, whether by virtue of race, ethnicity, sexual orientation, or gender identity. I wanted to provide opportunities for publication to folks who did not have classic po-biz credentials. But you know what? By that time, virtually all poetry presses were clamoring for work by poets from marginalized groups. Women, people of color, LGBTQ poets, nonbinary poets, intersex poets, undocumented poets, poets with HIV, poets with histories of trauma or mental illness—They did not really need Indolent Books to look out for their interests. So these days, I publish who and what I want to publish, plain and simple. I remain committed to inclusion, but I'm no longer looking over my shoulder for the inclusivity police. For me, and for Indolent Books, inclusion is a given—or at least, it should be. Gives a whole new meaning to the phrase, *poetic justice*.

MICHAEL BRODER